MEXICO
BEAUTIFUL LAND
DIVERSE PEOPLE

THE GULF STATES
OF MEXICO

RANDI FIELD

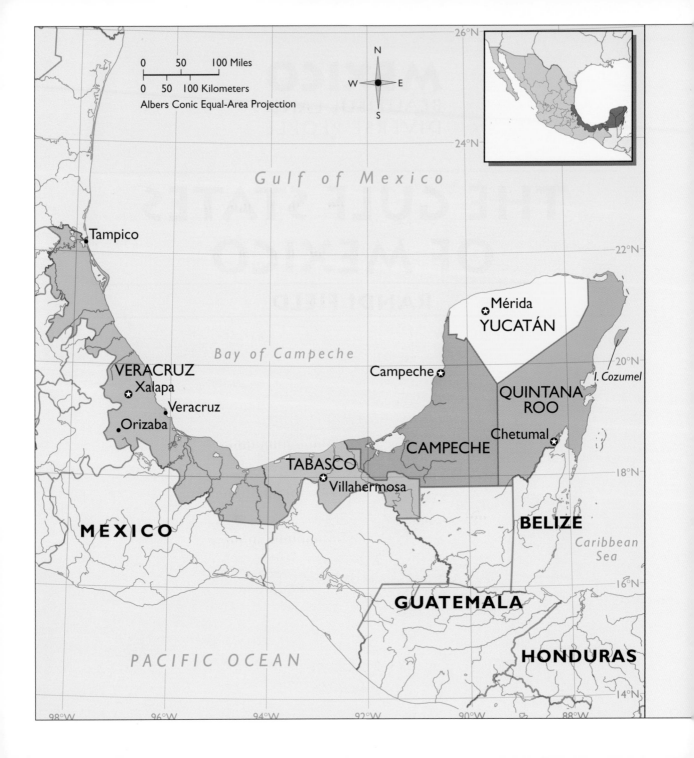

0   50   100 Miles

0   50   100 Kilometers

Albers Conic Equal-Area Projection

N
W   E
S

26°N

24°N

22°N

20°N

18°N

16°N

14°N

Gulf of Mexico

Tampico

Bay of Campeche

VERACRUZ

Xalapa

Veracruz

Orizaba

MEXICO

TABASCO

Villahermosa

Mérida
YUCATÁN

Campeche

QUINTANA
ROO

CAMPECHE

Chetumal

I. Cozumel

BELIZE

*Caribbean
Sea*

GUATEMALA

HONDURAS

PACIFIC OCEAN

98°W   96°W   94°W   92°W   90°W   88°W

MEXICO
BEAUTIFUL LAND
DIVERSE PEOPLE

THE GULF STATES OF MEXICO

RANDI FIELD

Mason Crest Publishers
Philadelphia

Mason Crest Publishers
370 Reed Road
Broomall PA 19008
www.masoncrest.com

First printing

1 3 5 7 9 8 6 4 2

Library of Congress Cataloging-in-Publication Data on file at the Library of Congress

Field, Randi.
    The Gulf states of Mexico / Randi Field.
        p. cm. — (Mexico—beautiful land, diverse people)
    Includes index.
    ISBN 978-1-4222-0668-3 (hardcover) — ISBN 978-1-4222-0735-2 (pbk.)
    1. Mexico—Juvenile literature. 2. Gulf Coast (Mexico)—Juvenile literature. I. Title.
    F1208.5.F54 2008
    972—dc22
                                          2008031860

TABLE OF CONTENTS

MEXICO
BEAUTIFUL LAND
DIVERSE PEOPLE

INTRODUCTION

exico is a country in the midst of great change. And what happens in Mexico reverberates in the United States, its neighbor to the north.

For outsiders, the most obvious of Mexico's recent changes has occurred in the political realm. From 1929 until the end of the 20th century, the country was ruled by a single political party: the Partido Revolucionario Institucional, or PRI (in English, the Institutional Revolutionary Party). Over the years, PRI governments became notorious for corruption, and the Mexican economy languished. In 2000, however, the PRI's stranglehold on national politics was broken with the election of Vicente Fox as Mexico's president. Fox, of the Partido de Acción Nacional (National Action Party), or PAN, promised political reform and economic development but had a mixed record as president. However, another PAN candidate, Felipe Calderón, succeeded Fox in 2006 after a hotly contested and highly controversial election. That election saw Calderón win by the slimmest of margins over a candidate from the Partido de la Revolución Democrática (Party of the Democratic Revolution). The days of one-party rule in Mexico, it seems, are gone for good.

Mexico's economy, like its politics, has seen significant changes in recent years. A 1994 free-trade agreement with the United States and Canada, along with the increasing transfer of industries from government control to private ownership under President Fox and President Calderón, has helped spur economic growth in Mexico. When all the world's countries are compared,

Mexico now falls into the upper-middle range in per-capita income. This means that, on average, Mexicans enjoy a higher standard of living than people in the majority of the world's countries. Yet averages can be misleading. In Mexico there is an enormous gap between haves and have-nots. According to some estimates, 40 percent of the country's more than 100 million people live in poverty. In some areas of Mexico, particularly in rural villages, jobs are almost nonexistent. This has driven millions of Mexicans to immigrate to the United States (with or without proper documentation) in search of a better life.

By 2006 more than 11 million people born in Mexico were living in the United States (including more than 6 million illegal immigrants), according to estimates based on data from the Pew Hispanic Center and the U.S. Census Bureau. Meanwhile, nearly one of every 10 people living in the United States was of Mexican ancestry. Clearly, Mexico and Mexicans have had—and will continue to have—a major influence on American society.

It is especially unfortunate, then, that many American students know little about their country's neighbor to the south. The books in the MEXICO: BEAUTIFUL LAND, DIVERSE PEOPLE series are designed to help correct that.

As readers will discover, Mexico boasts a rich, vibrant culture that is a blend of indigenous and European—especially Spanish—influences. More than 3,000 years ago, the Olmec people created a complex society and built imposing monuments that survive to this day in the Mexican states of Tabasco and Veracruz. In the fifth century A.D., when the Roman Empire collapsed and Europe entered its so-called Dark Age, the Mayan civilization was already flourishing in the jungles of the Yucatán Peninsula—and it would enjoy another four centuries of tremendous cultural achievements. By the time the Spanish conqueror Hernán Cortés landed at Veracruz in 1519, another great indigenous civilization, the Aztecs, had emerged to dominate much of Mexico.

With a force of about 500 soldiers, plus a few horses and cannons, Cortés marched inland toward the Aztec capital, Tenochtitlán. Built in the middle of a lake in what is now Mexico City, Tenochtitlán was an engineering marvel and one of the largest cities anywhere in the world at the time. With allies from among the indigenous peoples who resented being ruled by the Aztecs—and aided by a smallpox epidemic—Cortés and the Spaniards managed to conquer the Aztec Empire in 1521 after a brutal fight that devastated Tenochtitlán.

It was in that destruction that modern Mexico was born. Spaniards married indigenous people, creating mestizo offspring—as well as a distinctive Mexican culture that was neither Spanish nor indigenous but combined elements of both.

Spain ruled Mexico for three centuries. After an unsuccessful revolution in 1810, Mexico finally won its independence in 1821.

But the newly born country continued to face many difficulties. Among them were bad rulers, beginning with a military officer named Agustín Iturbide, who had himself crowned emperor only a year after Mexico threw off the yoke of Spain. In 1848 Mexico lost a war with the United States—and was forced to give up almost half of its territory as a result. During the 1860s French forces invaded Mexico and installed a puppet emperor. While Mexico regained its independence in 1867 under national hero Benito Juárez, the long dictatorship of Porfirio Díaz would soon follow.

Díaz was overthrown in a revolution that began in 1910, but Mexico would be racked by fighting until the Partido Revolucionario Institucional took over in 1929. The PRI brought stability and economic progress, but its rule became increasingly corrupt.

Today, with the PRI's long monopoly on power swept away, Mexico stands on the brink of a new era. Difficult problems such as entrenched inequalities and grinding poverty remain. But progress toward a more open political system may lead to economic and social progress as well. Mexico—a land with a rich and ancient heritage—may emerge as one of the 21st century's most inspiring success stories.

Tropical fish swim through a coral reef off the coast of Mexico's Yucatán peninsula. Tourism is an important part of Mexico's economy, as foreign visitors come to see the country's clear waters and sun-drenched beaches, ancient Indian ruins, and steaming jungles.

THE LAND

Imagine you're about to make your first visit to Mexico, also known as the United Mexican States. Your travels will take you to five states along the Gulf of Mexico: Tabasco, Veracruz, Campeche, Yucatán, and Quintana Roo.

The name Tabasco comes from a Nahuatl word meaning "waterlogged earth." The state's low plains are dotted with lakes and swamps, crossed by rivers, and covered in dense jungle. Tabasco has almost one-third of Mexico's water resources. The Grijalva River and the Usumacinta River, Mexico's largest rivers, flow through the state. The state has so few rocks that the Olmecs had to travel several miles to find material for the colossal heads that are still scattered across this state. Tabasco and Campeche contain Mexico's only rainforests.

Veracruz has the longest coastline of the Gulf states and is Mexico's 10th largest state. Its *tropical* land is filled with wooded areas, valleys, jungles, and over 40 rivers. About 35 percent of Mexico's rivers flow across the land. The Sierra Madre Oriental range and the Sierra Volcánica Transversal form a group of highlands. The Sierra Madre Oriental range

The Spanish castle of San Juan de Ulúa overlooks the harbor at Veracruz. It was built in 1528 to protect the harbor from Caribbean pirates. Veracruz was the first city founded by Europeans on the American mainland. Today, it is Mexico's largest and most important seaport.

includes Pico de Orizaba, Mexico's tallest peak. There is year-round snow on the highest peaks.

Campeche is an ideal place to enjoy a new type of tourism in Mexico called *ecotourism*, a mixture of ecology (caring for the environment), adventure, and history. The land is a dry plain to the north but green and tropical to the south where abundant lakes and rivers flow. Thick rainforest covers the south and eastern parts of the state. The water

Xcaret, an eco-archaeological park located on the Riviera Maya in Quintana Roo, also offers water sports. The park is about 45 miles south of Cancún.

along the coast is filled with barracuda, swordfish, tuna, and dolphins. Bird watchers can enjoy flamingos, parrots, and herons. A short distance from the coast, small hills give rise to low mountains.

Yucatán is covered with a flat, porous, limestone surface. There are no rivers on the surface, because rainwater filters through the porous surface. However, underground rivers have built caverns and *cenotes* (deep wells), mostly in the center and western part of the state. Near the white beaches along the turquoise coasts are many **lagoons** and sandbanks. Yucatán's green jungles surround the remains of the Mayan culture.

Quintana Roo is Mexico's youngest and 19th-largest state. A visit here is like a trip to paradise. White beaches are guarded by a chain of *coral reefs* in the turquoise and dark blue waters of the Caribbean Sea. The state includes the beautiful islands of Cozumel and Isla Mujeres. The state's most important river is the Hondo. There also are many blue lagoons and underground cenotes.

Don't miss the Sian Ka'an Biosphere Reserve on your visit. The 1.3-million–acre reserve was established by the Mexican government in

Uxmal, in Yucatán, is the site of important Mayan ruins. These ancient buildings, and the ones at nearby Chichén Itzá, draw many visitors to the state each year.

1986. It covers 10 percent of the state's land and includes 62 miles (100 kilometers) of coast. The reserve has lagoons, swamps, grasslands, forests, cenotes, and 70 miles of coral reef. It is home to hundreds of species of birds, fish, animals and plants as well as Mayan sites.

Cancún has become Mexico's most popular vacation spot. Hundreds of thousands of people visit the resort each year. In addition to scuba diving, which this tourist is enjoying, visitors to Cancún can try jet skiing, parachuting, scuba diving, fishing, water skiing, and snorkeling, take jungle tours, watch bullfights, or just enjoy the sunny, sandy beaches.

TABASCO

Location: Southeast Mexico.

Boundaries: the Gulf of Mexico (north), Campeche (northeast), the country of Guatemala (southeast), the state of Chiapas (south), and Veracruz (west).

Capital: Villahermosa

Total Area: 9,756 sq. miles (25,267 sq. kilometers)

Climate: Hot and humid with heavy rainfall.

Terrain: Low plains with a few highlands

Elevation: Main hills are the Madrigal, La Campana, Corona, and the Tortuguero in the Chiapas Sierra, a mountain range to low, flat plains at sea level.

Natural hazards: Flooding.

VERACRUZ

Location: Eastern Mexico.

Boundaries: the state of Tamaulipas (north); the states of Oaxaca and Chiapas (south); the Gulf of Mexico (east); the states of Puebla, San Luis Potosí, and Hidalgo (west); and Tabasco (southeast).

Capital: Jalapa

Total Area: 44,453 sq. miles (71,699 sq km.)
Coast length: 463 miles (745 km.)

Climate: Variable weather. Warm and humid over the coastline, humid in the jungle, and cooler in the high plains and mountains.

Terrain: Flat coastline, high plains, canyons, and mountains.

Elevation: Pico de Orizaba is 18,855 feet (5,747 meters above sea level) to flat coastline at sea level.

Natural hazards: Flooding, cyclones.

CAMPECHE

Location: Southeast Mexico.

Boundaries: Yucatán (north), Quintana Roo and the country of Belize (east), the country of Guatemala (south), and Tabasco and the Gulf of Mexico (west).

Capital: Campeche

Total Area: 19,619 sq. miles (50,812 sq km)

Climate: Hot and humid with a dry season in winter. The north is dry but the south can receive 60 inches of rain each year.

Terrain: Flatlands in the northeast and mountains in the south. Jungle filled with mahogany and cedar trees covers 60 percent of the land.

Elevation: 990 feet (300 meters) above sea level to flat plain at sea level.

Natural hazards: Hurricanes.

YUCATÁN

Location: Southern Mexico.

Boundaries: the Gulf of Mexico (north), Quintana Roo (east and southeast), and Campeche (west and southwest).

Capital: Mérida

Total Area: 14,827 sq. miles (38,402 sq km.)

Climate: The climate is hot and humid. The temperature cools when it rains or is windy.

Terrain Flat plains with a few hills.

Elevation: The Puuc Hills are about 100 meters or 328 feet tall to flat limestone surface at sea level.

Natural hazards: Hurricanes.

QUINTANA ROO

Location: Southern Mexico.

Boundaries: the Caribbean Sea (north and east), the countries of Belize and Guatemala (south), and Campeche and Yucatán (west).

Capital: Chetumal

Total Area: 19,387 sq. miles (50,212 sq km.)

Climate: Hot and humid with plentiful rain.

Terrain: Mostly flat plain. There are two main regions: the coastline and the inland area, where low jungle predominates.

Elevation: The flat plain is barely broken by a small hill 754 feet high, called "El Charro."

Natural hazards: Hurricanes, flooding.

THE HISTORY

Since this is your first visit to Mexico, you are in for many surprises. You may have seen pictures of ancient ruins and crystal clear waters in travel brochures, but no photograph could do justice to the archeological treasures left behind by Mexico's ancient peoples, As you touch a huge stone head in La Venta Park in Tabasco, you wonder, Who once lived here? How did they live? What were they like?

Mexican civilization began about 1150 B.C. with the Olmec Indians, Mexico's most ancient civilization. All of Mexico's later civilizations were influenced by the Olmecs. Tabasco and southern Veracruz have been called the Olmec heartland. This is where the civilization began and where its highest development took place.

Most of the Olmecs were *maize* (corn) farmers who also fished and hunted. They developed large-scale building methods and turned small agricultural villages into complex towns. Organized labor built ceremonial centers, and they were stone carvers who had their own style of art. The

This statue, found on the Yucatán Peninsula, depicts Chac Mool—an intermediary between the human and divine world. The Maya people would place offerings to the gods on the statue's stomach.

Olmecs also carved gigantic heads; some weighed several tons. The heads glorified their rulers when they were alive and commemorated them when they died. The Olmecs were one of the first civilizations with a written form of communication, **hieroglyphic** writing system. They also developed a calendar and system of numbering.

The Olmec people believed in a spirit world that caused their crops to die or grow. To please the spirit world, the Olmec practiced human sacrifice. They also invented a brutal, ceremonial game played throughout **Mesoamerica**. Teams represented opposing religious groups. The object of the ballgame was to hit a hard rubber ball through a ring hung high on the court walls. Like modern-day soccer, players could not use their hands. They had to hit the ball with another part of their bodies. Unlike modern games, the loser was put to death.

The Totonac Indians, a smaller Mexican civilization, lived in northern Veracruz. El Tajín, the Totonac word for "thunder," was the largest and most important city from A.D. 600 to 900. It thrived as a center for religion, art, architecture, and engineering. Hundreds of structures were built, including temples, palaces, walls, ball courts, and houses. The Totonacs who stayed in the area were conquered by the Aztec Indians in the late 15th century and forced to join the Aztec federation.

The Mayan civilization was one of the most important cultures in Mesoamerica. The culture grew in the area of the Mexican states of Tabasco, Yucatán, Campeche, Quintana Roo, Chiapas, and four Central American countries: Belize, Guatemala, El Salvador, and Honduras.

Mayan agricultural society began around 1000 B.C. By about 400 B.C., the people in the southern Yucatán Peninsula began turning farming and

20

Olmec artifacts, including the large stone carved head to the left, are on display at the La Venta Museum. The Olmecs created Mexico's first civilization more than 3,000 years ago.

trading villages into ceremonial centers that grew into complex cities. Large-scale agriculture and trade paved the way for social diversity.

The Maya were knowledgeable in science and math. They created a hieroglyphic writing system and recorded their history in books called codices. Their writing system is one of the most complex systems invented by any civilization. Record keeping and calculations were based on a mathematical system that included a symbol for zero.

Calendars were used to record historical dates and track astronomical events. The calendar system was based on the movements of the sun, moon, and the planet Venus. The Maya viewed the stars and planets as gods, and they built observatories to track their movements.

The Maya used different farming techniques. To prevent soil from wearing away, they terraced hillsides into levels. They also dug drainage channels and piled the soil they dug into rich mounds many feet high.

The channels allowed the Maya to get to their fields by boat and provided a steady supply of fish. When water shortages were a problem, the Maya built large-scale irrigation systems.

As arts and architecture grew with the economy, the Maya built steep pyramids, stone ball courts, and arched palaces. Paintings and sculptures show that the Mayan religion included opposing gods. Chac, the rain god, and Kukulcán (called Quetzalcoatl by the Toltecs), a friendly god, were the main deities. The Maya believed that royal families were descended from the gods, and the ruling class performed rituals showing their loyalty to the gods. Human sacrifices were made to soothe the gods during times of famine, plague or drought. Like the Olmecs and Totonacs, the Maya played brutal ballgames.

At its peak, the Mayan civilization grew to about 10 or 20 million people. As many as 200 large cities may have existed, some with populations over 50,000.

By A.D. 900, the civilization started to decline. In its final years, the society collapsed into warring political groups. Historians believe that over-population, the destruction of natural resources, and greedy rulers may have caused the decline. By around 1450, most cities had collapsed.

The end of the world the Maya knew came when the Spanish *conquistadors* arrived in the Americas in the 16th century. Set on conquering the New World, the Spaniards came to find gold and jewels and convert the natives to Christianity.

The Spanish made three important discovery expeditions. In 1517, Francisco Hernández de Córdoba sailed from Cuba looking for slaves to

work in Spanish mines. He landed on an island that is part of present-day Quintana Roo. There he found a stone temple and hundreds of figurines of women representing Ixchel, the fertility goddess, and her daughters. Córdoba named the island *Isla Mujeres* ("Island of Woman").

The Spanish asked the Mayan villagers the name of the land, but the only syllables the Spanish caught were "uhuuthaan," which means "listen how they speak." Thinking the villagers were saying the name of the area, the Spanish called the region Yucatán. The Spaniards looted temples and stole gold ornaments, then traveled to the mainland. They were attacked by Mayan warriors and fled to their base on Cuba, but the damage was done—the Spanish now knew of the riches to be claimed for the Spanish crown, and they would return.

Córdoba died from wounds caused by the Maya, but Juan de Grijalva continued his explorations. In 1518, Grijalva covered the same ground as Córdoba but kept going and discovered a huge river in the state of Tabasco. The river was later named after him, and today, the Grijalva River crosses Villahermosa, the state capital.

In 1519, Hernán Cortés sailed from Cuba and landed on the coast of Tabasco, where he won a battle with the natives. As a reward for his victory, the chiefs gave him 20 slave women. One woman was named La Malinche. Called Doña Marina by the Spaniards, she had been born an Aztec but had been sold into slavery and wound up in Tabasco. She learned the Mayan language spoken in the Yucatán but kept her knowledge of Nahuatl, the language spoken by the Aztecs and most non-Mayan Indians. Her understanding of Indian languages was very helpful to Cortés.

Cortés learned about the Aztec empire and its ruler, Montezuma II,

The conquistador Juan de Grijalva, a nephew of the Spanish colonial governor of Cuba, Diego Velázquez, explored the east coast of Mexico for Spain. His adventures paved the way for Hernán Cortés's conquest of the Aztec empire and the eventual settlement of New Spain.

from the Tabascans. The Aztec Indians lived in Central and Southern Mexico. They had created a huge empire by conquering other Indian nations.

The Spaniards moved to present-day Veracruz, where they established a town, making it the first European city settled in North America. Here Cortés met the Totonac Indians. Conquered by the Aztecs in 1450, the Totonacs despised the Aztecs for forcing them to perform human sacrifices to the Aztec war god. The Totonacs got revenge by forming an alliance with Cortés. They were glad to assist an Aztec enemy and lent Cortés soldiers and supplies.

The alliance enlarged Cortés's army and encouraged him to continue toward the Aztec capital of Tenochtitlán to fight the Aztecs. On his march, he faced opposition from the Tlaxcaltecan Indians. After three weeks of combat, these Indians also joined Cortés. Doña Marina helped Cortés negotiate a treaty with the Indians.

The combined forces marched to Tenochtitlán. In 1520, Montezuma was killed, and the next year Cortés and his Indian allies destroyed Tenochtitlán, the capital of the Aztec empire.

Spain's conquest of New Spain (Mexico, Central America, Florida, and the Caribbean Islands) was a disaster for the Native Americans, including those living along the Gulf Coast. The Spanish tried to destroy their religion and convert them to Christianity. Temples were torn down. Shrines were destroyed. Mayan expertise in math and astronomy withered. Only European-style writing was allowed and knowledge of the hieroglyphs faded.

War and epidemics of European diseases, such as measles, **smallpox**, and influenza, killed millions of Maya who had no **immunities** against the diseases. Most survivors were stripped of their lands and treated like slaves. They were forced to work on Spanish estates. Several native rebellions took place during the Spanish conquest because of the terrible conditions created by the Spaniards, but by 1547, the conquest of the Yucatán Peninsula was mostly complete. Since the Spaniards could not understand the Mayan language, they renamed most places. This is why today few Mayan names exist on the Yucatán Peninsula.

New Spain was ruled by Spain for 300 years. During this time, Mexico's natural riches were discovered and taken by the Spaniards. A **caste system** developed that divided the people into social classes. Spaniards born in Spain were in the highest class. They usually came from nobility and held high-ranking government jobs. Next came those born in Mexico whose parents were Spanish. Many became landowners and merchants. Unions between Indian women and Spaniards created a class of mixed-blood people called *mestizos*. They were considered inferior by the pureblood Spaniards.

Native Americans were in the lowest class. They were put to work building chapels, cathedrals, convents, and palaces for their Spanish masters. The Mexican-born Spaniards enjoyed comfortable lives by forcing the Indians to run their farms, ranches, mines, and business ventures. Hundreds of thousands of Native Americans were worked to death. Others died from disease. When the loss of much of the Indian population created a huge labor shortage, the Spanish solved the problem by importing African slaves.

The port of Veracruz became the entrance to New Spain and an important means of communication between Spain and New Spain. The route between Veracruz and Mexico City was vital for commerce. Towns along this route flourished. The Spanish discovered the delicious vanilla growing in a town near the port of Veracruz and named the area Papantla, which means "Vanilla Town."

The Yucatán Peninsula became a refuge for pirates. Once called "Ah Kin Pech," a Mayan name meaning "Place of the Serpents and Ticks," the city of Campeche was renamed by the Spanish. The city became another important port for New Spain. For this reason, it was attacked by pirates looking for treasure during the 17th and 18th centuries. For protection, a huge wall was built around the city. The wall was 24 feet high, six feet wide, and over 1,800 square feet long.

The coastal area of Tabasco also suffered several attacks from pirates. The inhabitants of a town named Villa de Santa María de la Victoria moved to San Juan Bautista in 1596 to escape attacks. Two

The house where Hernán Cortés lived after his conquest of the Aztec empire is still standing in Antigua. The home was built in 1525.

years later, they changed the city's name to Villahermosa. In 1641, Tabasco's government was established in Villahermosa. *Cacao* crops were grown, and trade developed in the area.

During Mexico's war for independence, several groups rebelled and opposed the Spanish forces when they arrived at the port of Veracruz. It was here that the last battles against the Spaniards took place. In 1821, General Agustín de Iturbide led an army of patriots into Mexico City and the last Spanish viceroy was forced to return to Spain.

The Treaty of Córdoba was signed, establishing Mexico's independence from Spain. Iturbide crowned himself emperor of Mexico, but he was *exiled* shortly afterward. General Antonio López de Santa Anna declared that Mexico was a *republic* on December 6, 1822.

28

When Santa Anna became president in 1832, he drained the country's treasury. Mexico was unable to pay its debts. The final straw came when a French pastry chief's goods were devoured by Mexican troops. France attacked Veracruz in what became known as the "Pastry War." The French were driven back and forced to accept a small payment for the debt.

During the early 1800s, many Americans moved to present-day Texas. The land was part of Mexico, and Santa Anna's troops stormed the area. The Texans won their freedom in 1836, and joined the United States in 1845. When Mexico disagreed over the Texas border, war was declared the next year. U. S. troops captured Veracruz in 1847. In 1848, the Treaty of Guadalupe Hidalgo was signed. The treaty returned Veracruz but forced Mexico to give up a large amount of land. The area included present-day Texas, Arizona, New Mexico, California, Nevada, Utah, and parts of Colorado and Oklahoma.

Although Yucatán avoided war during the struggle for independence, in later years attempts were made to separate the state from Mexico. The Caste War was fought from 1847 to 1904. It was the largest and most successful of Mexico's native rebellions and played an important part in the Yucatán Peninsula's history. Many factors sparked the war.

The Yucatecans, the ruling class, exercised control over the Mayan Indians. Mayan rebels struggled to retain their lands as more lands were taken over. A rebellion in Tepich (in present-day Quintana Roo) ignited the bloody conflict.

As the main port for the largest city in the Americas, Veracruz was the center of many battles during the Mexican War for Independence.

The Maya attacked Yucatán cities and towns, spreading terror and death. Just when the Maya were about to drive the Yucatecans from the peninsula, rain came, signaling the start of the planting season. The Maya put down their weapons and returned to their fields to grow corn. The Yucatecan army regrouped and attacked the rebels, regaining control of many cities. As the Yucatecan army advanced, many Maya were killed.

By 1850, the Maya rebels were on the brink of defeat. They hid in the jungles of Quintana Roo and started small communities. Believing they saw a talking cross, they renamed themselves the Cruzoob (followers of the cross). The place where the cross appeared, Chan Santa Cruz ("Small Holy Cross"), became an important rebel sanctuary for nearly 50 years.

In 1901, General Ignacio Bravo and his troops entered Chan Santa Cruz. The town fell under his control and the Mayan capital was renamed Santa Cruz de Bravo in honor of the general. The war was officially over three years later. Today, the town is known as Felipe Carrillo Puerto.

After Santa Anna gave up half of Mexico to the United States, Benito Juárez, a Zapotec Indian, seized leadership of the country. Juárez served as president from 1858 until his death in 1872. That same year, the Mexico City–Veracruz railway was completed.

From 1876 until 1910, General Porfirio Díaz held the presidency. Díaz was a dictator with complete power. Although modernization took place during his rule, most Mexicans were worse off than during Spanish rule. Foreigners owned many factories, transportation systems, and mines. Most land was owned by a handful of Mexican families.

A young Mexican man paddles a boat on a stream clogged with pollution from an oil refinery near the Pemex center in La Venta, Tabasco. Runoff from the plant, which separates crude oil from water and gas, has blighted a once-virgin swamp.

Mexicans worked for foreigners and landowners under terrible conditions. They were underfed, underpaid, and overworked.

Yucatán enjoyed economic growth, due to the henequen boom. Henequen, a natural fiber plant also known as sisal, is used to make ropes, bags, hammocks, hats, and other products. The industry's growth resulted in railway construction and other services. However, only a small group reaped the benefits from the boom and several rebellions took place.

Opposition to Díaz's government grew. In 1910, Francisco Madero urged all Mexicans to rebel. Uprisings grew until the whole country was in revolt. In the Gulf State region, a major rebel force of over 1,000 people took over the city of Valladolid, Yucatán. The rebels were crushed and their leaders were killed. Violence also broke out in Veracruz and continued until the mid-1920s.

In 1911, revolutionary generals Pascual Orozco and Pancho Villa captured the northern city of Ciudad Juárez, named after Benito

Juárez. Days later, Díaz resigned and fled the country. Madero became president but was betrayed by Victoriano Huerta, one of his generals, who ordered Madero's death. Huerta became the new dictator. In 1914, he too was overthrown. Finally, in 1917, a Mexican **constitution** was adopted establishing a democratic government run by the people. General Álvaro Obregón became president in 1920.

During Díaz's reign, the southern states had barely been touched by the modernization that occurred throughout the rest of Mexico. Felipe Carrillo Puerto, a socialist who believed in shared ownership of the state, became the governor of Yucatán in 1922. Two years later, followers of the Huerta rebellion killed him. Since then, the state's political and social life has been mostly calm. In 1959, President Mateos visited the city of Chetumal, Quintana Roo, and a new period of economic and social growth began that resulted in statehood in 1974.

Veracruz became the birthplace of the union movement when a group of oil workers went on strike in 1937. The strike ended in government control of the crude oil industry. Veracruz has experienced economic growth and social integration since that time.

Tabasco's growth was spurred by the discovery of oil about 50 years ago. The state-owned Pemex oil company brought modernization, and Tabasco had an oil boom in the 1980s. However, in the 1990s, oil well occupations created many disruptions. The Chontal Indians (Mayan descendents) and members of the state's Democratic Revolutionary Party blocked entrances to Pemex. Occupiers protested Pemex's plans to dig more wells and demanded compensation for farmers for damage done to the environment from oil operations.

A man carries a load of henequen leaves on his shoulders in the Yucatán peninsula. Fibers from the henequen plant are used to make ropes, bags, hammocks, hats, and other products.

THE ECONOMY

During your visit, you'll find that Mexico is a poor country. Its average *per capita income* in 2007 was $7,870. As in the past, there is a huge gap between the rich and the poor.

Tabasco is one of Mexico's main oil-producing areas. Its growing manufacturing industry produces *petrochemicals* and oil by-products. Products made from petrochemicals include plastics, soaps, fertilizer, and paint. The oil industry's growth helped modernize the state, but *shantytowns* fill the state side by side with the refineries.

Modern machinery and methods have helped agricultural activities. The most important crops are cacao, coconut, sugarcane, bananas, pepper, and rubber. Tabasco is Mexico's largest cacao producer. On your trip, you could visit a sugarcane factory or a cacao plantation. Other important industries are fishing, mining, tourism, and trade.

Tabascans make handicraft products from cedar and mahogany woods, including furniture, carved masks, and drums. Their specialty is products made from wild animal skins such as shoes and purses made from iguana or alligator. Textile production includes making shirts, embroidered napkins, and mosquito nets.

The seeds of the cacao tree are used to produce cocoa and chocolate. Cacao trees are grown throughout the Gulf states region, although Tabasco is the largest producer.

The discovery of oil in Veracruz caused a population explosion in the state. The population grew from one million at the beginning of the century to about 7 million people today, making Veracruz the third most populated state in Mexico. The state has over one-fourth of Mexico's petroleum reserves and is one of Mexico's main oil producers. It supplies 17 percent of Mexico's energy and is the second-largest generator of electricity after Chiapas. Laguna Verde, the country's only nuclear electric power plant, is located here.

Fishing is another major activity. The fishing fleet is the largest in Mexico, and the oyster catch is among the country's highest. Veracruz is Mexico's fifth largest producer in the manufacturing sector. Vital industries include textiles, fertilizers, pesticides, paper, iron and steel, and engineering. Important agricultural products are corn, sugarcane, beans, coffee, mango, rice, tobacco, papaya, mangos, bananas, pineapples, and oranges. Veracruz is Mexico's leading coffee, rice, and meat producer.

Vanilla plants are grown in Papantla. Another important industry is built around the tourists who visit the state's historical sites and ancient ruins.

Many Maya live on the Yucatán Peninsula today. They live in small villages and grow corn, citrus, and vegetables. They also fish and weave hammocks. However, more and more workers are finding jobs in the big cities where the tourism industry thrives. They find restaurant work, weave hammocks for tourists, and act as guides at archeological sites. The Maya are skilled artisans. They make many items from cotton, wood, clay, sisal, and palm such as purses, hats, baskets, sandals, shoes, tablecloths, slippers, and belts. Combs and hair ornaments are made from tortoiseshell.

Campeche is another one of Mexico's leading oil producers due to its closeness to offshore oil fields in the Bay of Campeche. Large petroleum deposits are under the bay. Major oil fields were developed

A craftsman carves the face of a guitar in Campeche. Although the region's industry is growing, many people still make their living from handcrafted items.

in the 1970s, and by the 1980s, the bay was the highest oil-producing area in the region. The city of Campeche is the bay's service center. Oil platforms dot the coast but most are concentrated near Ciudad del Carmen at the western end of the state. The state also accounts for 26.5 percent of Mexico's natural gas production.

Campeche's landscape is good for agriculture, fishing, and forestry. Most agriculture is done in the south. Major crops are rice, corn, sugarcane, and fruit. Better irrigation systems have increased rice production. Beekeeping activities have shown constant growth, and Campeche's shrimp catch is among the highest in Mexico. About 14 percent of the economy is based on wood and wood products. Campeche specialties include wooden furniture, tortoiseshell and coral handicrafts, pottery, and sisal production. Tourism is developing as archeological sites become better known.

For years, the lack of roads and communications systems kept the Yucatán Peninsula from developing with the rest of Mexico. Recently, good highways and other changes have helped economic growth in the area. The restoration of old Mayan sites, such as Chichén Itzá and Uxmal, and the development of railroad, highway, and air connections to bring visitors have made tourism the most important economic activity. On your visit, you'll enjoy Yucatecan food, Mayan ruins, the Caribbean coastline, tourist facilities, and handicrafts.

Citrus fruit, sisal, vegetables, and corn are Yucatán's main crops. Vegetables grown include chili peppers, tomatoes, and cantaloupes. The state's beekeeping activities have made it one of the world's leading honey producers. Fishing, forestry, industry, and commerce are also

Mayan ruins at Tulum overlook the sea. Tourism is Quintana Roo's major source of revenue.

vital. Companies operate in many industries, including textiles and apparel, jewelry, electronics, toys, and furniture.

Because of its amazing Mayan ruins and modern resorts, such as Cancún, Cozumel, Isla Mujeres, Chetumal, and Playa del Carmen, Quintana Roo's leading industry is tourism. The state generates 25 percent of Mexico's foreign earnings from tourism. Tropical forests cover almost one-third of the state, and it is one of Mexico's leading fine wood producers. Other important industries are fishing, cattle raising, factories, trade, and

A shrimp boat fishes the waters off the coast of Mexico. Shrimp fishing is one of the important industries in Campeche.

agriculture. Citrus fruits and coconuts are among the main agricultural products, and the variety of sea species makes fishing popular. The government has created a strong ecotourism program because of the state's important ecological and archeological sites.

In January 1994, the North American Free Trade Agreement (NAFTA) went into effect between Mexico, Canada, and the United States. The agreement eliminates restrictions, such as *tariffs*, on the flow of goods, services, and investments. It allows free trade between the countries.

NAFTA has helped the *maquiladora* industry in the Gulf states. A maquiladora is a Mexican company that is allowed to import duty-free (without tax) the materials and equipment needed to produce goods. Most maquiladoras produce electronics, textiles, or auto parts and accessories. Recently, maquiladoras have caused international concern because of the unsafe and unfair working conditions that exist in many of these factories. Maquiladoras, do however, help bring foreign investment to the Gulf states.

THE GULF STATES OF MEXICO

40

TABASCO

*Per capita income
in pesos:* 8,543

Natural resources: Oil,
sugar, cacao

*GDP in thousands of
pesos:* 16,140,535

Percentage of GDP:
Manufacturing 9%
Commerce 23%
Service industries 62%
Other 6%

Exports:
Oil, petrochemicals,
sugar, and coffee

VERACRUZ

*Per capita income
in pesos:* 8,636

Natural resources: Oil,
sulpur, kaolin, silica,
coffee, fruit, and fish

*GDP in thousands of
pesos:* 59,594,896

Percentage of GDP:
Manufacturing 17%
Commerce 25%
Service industries 53%
Other 5%

Exports:
Iron and steel, plastics,
machinery, organic and
inorganic chemicals,
natural fertilizers, coffee,
tea, sugar, limes, vinegar,
tobacco, and oil.

CAMPECHE

*Per capita income
in pesos:* 21,586

Natural resources: Oil,
wood, fish and
crustaceans

*GDP in thousands of
pesos:* 48,992,496

Percentage of GDP:
Manufacturing 11%
Commerce 54%
Service industries 35%

Exports:
Oil, fishery, marine
products, honey, textiles,
and tanning extracts

YUCATÁN

*Per capita income
in pesos:* 11,128

Natural resources: Sisal, citrus, bees, fish, wood

GDP in thousands of pesos: 56,711,465

Percentage of GDP:
Manufacturing 17%
Commerce 43%
Service industries 38%
Other 2%

Exports:
Textiles and apparel, honey, seafood, handicrafts, orange juice concentrate, furniture and wood products, fruits, vegetables, limestone and marble.

QUINTANA ROO

*Per capita income
in pesos:* 21,294

Natural resources: Wood, citrus fruits, coconuts, fish and crustaceans

GDP in thousands of pesos: 56,809,650

Percentage of GDP:
Manufacturing 8%
Commerce 47%
Service industries 44%
Other 1%

Exports:
Sugar, molasses, honey, shellfish, watermelon, coconuts, calcite, and chicle (for chewing gum)

PER CAPITA INCOME = the amount earned in an area divided by the total number of people living in that area

GDP = Gross Domestic Product, the total value of goods and services produced during the year

1 PESO = about $0.11, as of January 2002

*Figures from INEGI,
the Mexican National Institute of Statistics, based on Mexico's 2000 census.*

A Mayan bungalow in Yucatán. Much of Mexico's culture today is *mestizo*—
a mixture of Spanish and native influences and traditions.

THE CULTURE

Most of Mexico's population is *mestizo*, a combination of Native American and Spanish. Spanish is the country's official language. However, the millions of Mayan people who make up a large part of the population on the Yucatán Peninsula still use native dialects. Mexico is mainly a Catholic country. Crosses, shrines, and churches are plentiful.

Most of Tabasco's people are either mestizos or Chontal Indians. The state's **cuisine** is based on Mayan recipes. The dishes use a lot of cacao since the state is Mexico's main cacao producer. There are exotic dishes too. For instance, if you ordered *torta de iguana*, you would be served iguana with parsley, chili, onion, and eggs baked on a banana leaf. *Balché*, a thick drink made from corn, was a ritual drink for the ancient Maya, and today, Chontales still offer balché to the earth, mountains, and goblins.

Tabascan women wear dark, flowered skirts and tops. The skirt is longer in the front and shorter in the back to allow more freedom to dance. Men in Tabasco and Veracruz wear white cotton pants and *guayaberas*, a cotton or silk shirt.

A mariachi group performs traditional Mexican folk music in Veracruz. Mariachi bands usually consist of musicians with stringed instruments like violins and guitars, and sometimes also include singers and musicians with brass instruments.

Traditional instruments such as drums and flutes are played to accompany the Mexican tap dance. The *El Pocho* is a dance that starts with a flour war in the town of Tenosique. Dancers throw flour at pedestrians who cross their path.

Every April, the state fair is celebrated in Villahermosa with livestock and crafts displays, parades, dance contests, and sporting events. The highlight is a beauty contest where the winner is crowned the most beautiful flower in the state.

Veracruz, the first European city in the Americas, is where the cultural mix between Native Americans and Spaniards began. About 10 percent of the people speak native languages. The state's Afro-Cuban influence comes from the days when the city of Veracruz was a main slave trading port for Mexico. The influence is found in the music, food, and population, especially in the city of Veracruz where **marimba** bands perform nightly with **mariachi** musicians nearby. Caribbean colors are prevalent. The *danzón*, an elegant, slow dance, is held three times a week. People of all ages gather at the Plaza de Armas to dance.

The Feast of Corpus Christi begins on June 1 in Papantla, one of the few remaining centers of Totonac culture. The 10-day festival celebrates native and Christian traditions with art expositions and fireworks. On Corpus Day, fliers enact the famous "Dance of the Flyers." The ancient Totonacs performed the ceremony every 52 years to ask their rain god to water the crops. Today, four fliers dance on a platform on top a high pole. The four points around the pole represent the sun, wind, moon, and earth. Then each flier rotates backward around the pole while tethered to it. Together they circle the pole 52 times to represent the Totanac cycle.

Both Spanish and Mayan dialects are spoken in Campeche. Natives of this state are very fond of music. They have frequent concerts, musical festivals, and regional dances. The women decorate their hair with tortoiseshell combs.

The state is also famous for its seafood. Shrimp, sea bass, red snapper,

A group of Mayans known as the Papantla Flyers performs at Tulum, Quintana Roo. They are reenacting an ancient Totonac ceremony intended to bring rain for farmers.

Folk dancers perform at a hotel in Mexico.

dogfish, octopus, squid and oysters are prepared in every imaginable way.

The country celebrates the Day of the Dead in November with a feast for the dead. Villages celebrate with special zest because it corresponds to a similar native tradition.

In February, the city of Campeche celebrates **Carnival** with floats, parades, dances, and costumes.

In Mérida, the capital of Yucatán, and in Progreso, the state's main port, the population is both mestizo and Mayan. In much of the rest of the state, the population is mostly Mayan. Many Maya do not speak any Spanish, mostly because the state is geographically isolated from the rest of Mexico.

Typical dances include the *okostapol* (head dance) and the *Bombas Yucatecas* (Bombs from Yucatán). The region's best music is the *jaranas*, a combination of native songs and popular music in a fast, happy rhythm.

The tropical waters of the Caribbean and Gulf of Mexico are a diver's paradise with hundreds of species of tropical fish. Jet skiing, parasailing, scuba diving, and snorkeling are among the area's water sports.

Quintana Roo is a mixture of cultures. The region around the country of Belize is about one-half African descent, one-quarter Maya, and one-quarter mestizo and white. Along the coast and Chetumal, there is a strong Caribbean influence, especially in the food, architecture, and music.

Central Quintana Roo, known as *Zona Maya*, has many rural communities where the Maya practice ancient customs mixed with Christian rituals. The Maya go to church—and they attend ceremonies held by the Mayan priest. One of the most important rituals is the *Cha chaac*, a request to the rain god to send water to the cornfields.

Other parts of the state are a mix of Spanish, Mayan, and foreigners. The Day of the Dead is an important holiday here, and the feast of Santa Cruz is celebrated in May with processions, bullfights, fireworks, and the "Dance of the Pig's Head." There are many recreational activities, since the state has large natural preservation areas, archeological zones, modern shopping centers, and beautiful landscapes to enjoy fishing and other water sports.

Spectators turn from a person costumed to represent death during Mexico's Day of the Dead celebration. The Day of the Dead is held to remember the souls of friends and family members who have passed away.

Two gardeners mow the lawns surrounding two pyramids at the Comalcalco site in Tabasco. Comalcalco was an important center of the ancient Mayan civilization.

THE CITIES AND COMMUNITIES

Villahermosa, with a population of 519,873, is Tabasco's modern capital, a huge city whose recent growth was spurred by oil discoveries during the past 50 years. The city is important to the economies of Tabasco and Chiapas because of the petroleum industry. Outstanding tourist attractions include the La Venta Museum with 33 Olmec heads, and the Carlos Pellicer Cámara Anthropology Museum with Olmec and Mayan artifacts and pictures. A newer attraction is the Yumka Nature Reserve. Its 250 acres of jungle, flat grassland, and wetlands provide a home to endangered or threatened species such as spider monkeys, toucans, crocodiles, and turtles.

Comalcalco (population 164,640) means "place of the clay griddles" in Nahuatl, and it is the oldest brick city in the Americas. It was an ancient Mayan *civic* and religious center, and the city is unique because the Chontal Maya did not have stones to build temples so they used baked clay. Designs of birds, reptiles, geometric shapes, hands, and feet were pressed in the bricks before they were baked. Daily events and practices were recorded on the bricks. Cortés learned about Comalcalco from Doña Marina, because the chiefs of the city had sold her into captivity. She got revenge when Cortés sacked the city. Many bricks from its temples were used to build colonial buildings and pave the streets, and Chontal descendants still live there. Tourists can visit cacao plantations and nearby chocolate factories.

Jalapa (or Xalapa), with a population of 390,058, is the capital of Veracruz. It was conquered by the Aztec Indians in 1460 and was part of the Aztec empire until 1519, when Cortés claimed the land for Spain. When Cortés arrived, it was a Totonac ceremonial center, but today it is a university town with a diverse population. Pretty flower gardens decorate its uneven streets. Its buildings have kept their colonial style, and the city has several impressive buildings, including the Government Palace and Anthropology Museum. This is one the best archeological museums in the Americas, with over 25,000 artifacts, including Olmec heads.

The city of Veracruz, officially Veracruz Llave (population 457,119), is the oldest port city in the Americas and the largest Mexican city on the Caribbean. It is one of Mexico's primary seaports and can handle 12 million tons of goods each year. The port is linked by highway and railroad to Mexico City, the nation's capital, and is a major commercial and manufacturing center. Streets are lined with old and new buildings. Attractions include museums, churches, and plazas where marimba bands play.

You may want to visit the Castillo de San Juan de Ulúa, a fortress built by the Spanish in 1528 to guard the harbor from Caribbean

This building in Mérida is a fine example of Spanish colonial architecture.

pirates. After 1825, the fort was used as a high-security jail for political prisoners. Benito Juárez was imprisoned there by Santa Anna before the dictator was exiled.

Córdoba (population 176,952), where the treaty ending Spanish rule was signed, was founded by the Spanish in 1618 as a stronghold against slave rebellions at sugarcane plantations. Today, Córdoba is an important distribution center for fruit, coffee, and tobacco.

The city of Campeche (population 216,735) is the state capital. Walled since 1686, the city has an historic downtown area. Its tourist attractions include a fort, a cathedral in the main plaza, the Botanical

An aerial photograph shows Plaza de Armas, in the center of Veracruz. This is the largest Mexican city on the Caribbean coast.

Garden, and, of course, its huge wall. Campeche and Champotón (population 80,224), founded by the Spanish in 1537, were among the first colonial settlements in the state.

Ciudad del Carmen, also known as *Isla del Carmen* (population 181,566), is a peaceful island city and the main shrimp port in Mexico. There is no colonial architecture here because English pirates ruled the island during colonial times. Apart from fishing, the people support themselves by making products from fine woods and alligator and sharkskin. It has beautiful beaches, a cypress forest, and the San Felipe Fort, built during the 17th century as a defense against pirates. The city was annexed to Campeche in 1863.

Mérida (population 703,324), Yucatán's state capital, is the largest city on the Yucatán Peninsula. Francisco de Montejo conquered the peninsula and founded Mérida in 1542 on top of the Mayan city of

The walls of a Spanish fort in Campeche, on the Yucatán Peninsula. Campeche is the state's largest city, and was the site of one of the first Spanish settlements in the region.

T'ho. Today, Mérida is an important business and educational center for southeastern Mexico. Known as the "White City" because it is so clean, the city is a mix of old and new buildings. It has a colonial atmosphere with mansions, a towering cathedral, museums, market places, and small churches. In the market area, you can buy handicrafts such as traditional clothing and sisal woven rugs. On Sundays, the main square is closed to traffic, and dancers perform for crowds.

Valladolid (population 56,742), founded in 1543 on the Mayan town of Sisal, is the second largest city in the state. During the Caste War and later the Mexican Revolution, the Maya revolted and killed most of the Spanish residents. Today, it is an agricultural market town with a colonial center. Tension still exists between the Spanish and Maya, however. As a visitor, you may hear Mayan spoken by women weaving, vendors on street corners, and around archeological sites.

Some 12 miles of beaches in Cancún are lined with luxury hotels. The popular resort has grown tremendously in the past 30 years. Today it is one of Mexico's largest cities.

Tizimín (population 63,993), a Mayan name meaning "site of the tapir," is the state's livestock center. Livestock and religious fairs are held here. Progreso (or Puerto Progreso, population 48,692) is Yucatán's main port and a federal pier. It is also a shelter for fishing fleets and sport boats.

Chetumal (population 208,014) is the capital of Quintana Roo, Mexico's youngest state. Located near the border with Belize, it has tropical weather and English-style wooden houses. The city was founded in 1898 to block arms shipments to Mayan rebels. A hurricane destroyed Chetumal in 1955, but the city was reconstructed with wide avenues, modern architecture, and a waterfront boulevard. It has a huge shopping district and a fine museum.

In 1967, the Mexican government did a study to find the ideal Caribbean resort. A computer chose Cancún (population 419,276).

Hacked out of the jungle over 30 years ago, Cancún's beaches, ancient ruins, and tourist services have made it one of the most famous tourist resorts in the world and Mexico's most popular resort. Luxury hotels line its 12 miles of white coastline. During the day, you can try just about any water sport, including jet skiing, parachuting, scuba diving, fishing, waterskiing, and snorkeling. You can also take jungle tours or walk along the turquoise sea. The city's bullring has bullfights all year long.

Cozumel is Mexico's largest inhabited island. According to a Mayan legend, Cozumel (population 60,025) was the sanctuary of Ixchel, the goddess of love and fertility. Temples were built to thank her for sending the Maya's favorite bird, the swallow. The island was named "the Island of the Swallows." The Spanish used Cozumel as a naval base in the late 16th century, and then, after a period of desertion, it became a 17th-century refuge for pirates like Francis Drake and Jean Lafitte. Palancar Reef, the world's second largest barrier reef, was discovered by French diver Jacques Cousteau in the 1961. The island was revitalized after Cousteau's discovery. Today, Cozumel's waters are a diver's paradise, with about 500 species of fish. It is Mexico's most popular diving destination and the country's biggest cruise-ship port.

For many years, Isla Mujeres (population 11,316) was a small fishing village. In the 1950s, vacationing Mexicans discovered the island with its peaceful beaches, and they were followed by other tourists. Some inhabitants there still earn a living by fishing, but most sell souvenirs and cater to tourists. While scuba diving in its waters, you can see the remains of sunken ships surrounded by reefs and colorful fish.

CHRONOLOGY

1150 B.C.	Mexican civilization begins with the Olmec Indians.
1000 B.C.	Mayan agricultural society begins.
1450	Aztecs conquer the Totonacs in Veracruz.
1518	Hernán Cortés lands on the coast of Tabasco.
1542	Mérida is founded by the Spanish.
1596	Villahermosa is settled by the Spanish.
1821	Mexico becomes independent from Spain.
1822	Tabasco becomes a state.
1847–1904	The Caste War is fought.
1863	Campeche becomes an independent state.
1872	Mexico City-Veracruz railway is completed.
1898	Chetumal is founded to block arms shipments to Mayan rebels.
1910–1921	Mexican Revolution.
1937	Birth of the union movement in Veracruz.
1974	Quintana Roo becomes a state.
2006	Archaeologists announce the discovery of a stone tablet in Veracruz, claiming it is probably Olmec and is the oldest known example of New World writing.
2007	Category 5 Hurricane Dean strikes the Yucatán Peninsula, forcing over 30,000 people to evacuate; widespread floods hit Tabasco and the neighboring state of Chiapas, killing several people.

FOR MORE INFORMATION

MEXICO

Mexican Secretariat of Tourism
http://www.mexonline.com/mxtur.htm

TABASCO

Government of Tabasco
http://www.tabasco.gob.mx

State Tourism Office
Av. Los Ríos s/n esq. Calle 13
Tabasco 2000
CP 86035 Villahermosa, Tabasco
Tel: (993) 316-5134
Fax: (993) 316-2890

VERACRUZ

Government of Veracruz
http://www.veracruz.gob.mx/

State Tourism Office
Blvd. Cristóbal Colón No. 5
CP 91190 Xalapa, Veracruz
Tel: (228) 812-8500
Fax: (228) 812-5939
E-mail:
ambiance_adventure@infosel.net.mx

CAMPECHE

Government of Campeche
http://www.campeche.gob.mx

State Tourism Office
Av. Ruiz Cortines s/n
Plaza Moch-Couoh Centro
CP 24000, Campeche, Campeche
Tel: (981) 811-9200
Fax: (981) 816-6068

YUCATÁN

Government of Yucatán
http://www.yucatan.gob.mx

State Tourism Office
Calle 59 No. 514 entre 62 y 64 Centro
CP 97000 Mérida, Yucatán
Tel: (999) 924-9389
Fax: (999) 928-6547

QUINTANA ROO

Government of Quintana Roo
http://www.quintanaroo.gob.mx

State Tourism Office
Carr. a Calderitas No. 622
Entre Ciricote e Ignacio Comonfort
CP 77010 Chetumal, Quintana Roo
Tel: (983) 835-0860
Fax: (983) 835-0880

57

GLOSSARY

Cacao The bean from which chocolate is made.

Carnival The celebration before Lent involving feasting, masquerading, and partying.

Caste system A system that divides people into classes according to their rank, wealth or profession, or that of the family into which they were born.

Civic Having to do with the rights or responsibilities of citizens or a city.

Conquistadors The Spanish conquerors of the New World.

Constitution The basic principles and laws of a nation.

Coral reefs Accumulations beneath the ocean of the skeletal remains of a sea creature.

Cuisine Manner of preparing food; cooking style.

Ecotourism A form of tourism that attempts to minimize ecological damage to areas visited for their natural or cultural interest.

Exiled Sent away from one's home or country.

Hieroglyphic Belonging to a system of writing that is made up of picture characters.

Immunities Conditions that allow a person to resist a particular disease.

Lagoons A shallow sound or lake that leads into the ocean or another body of water.

Mariachi Mexican street band.

Marimba A xylophone originally from southern Africa with resonators beneath each bar.

Mesoamerica   The region of southern North America that was inhabited before the coming of Columbus.

Per capita income   The amount earned in an area divided by the number of people living in that area.

Petrochemicals   Chemicals made from petroleum or oil.

Republic   A government where the power belongs to a body of citizens who elect their officials.

Shantytowns   Settlements made up of shacks.

Smallpox   A contagious disease that causes high fevers and pus-filled sores that leave deep scars.

Tariff   A tax levied by the government on imported goods.

Tropical   Characteristic of a region or climate that is always frost-free, with temperatures warm enough and enough moisture to support year-round plant life.

THINGS TO DO AND SEE

TABASCO

Ancient Olmec ruins at La Venta Park in Villahermosa

Comalcalco archaeological zone and museum

Yumka nature reserve

VERACRUZ

Ancient Olmec ruins at San Lorenzo

Papantla's flying dancers

El Tajín's Totonac architecture

Cempoala's stone structures

Castillo de San Juan de Ulúa, the Spanish fort

CAMPECHE

Archaeological cities including Edzna, Rio Bec, Jaina, and Ixtampac

The huge wall surrounding the city of Campeche

YUCATÁN

Mayan ruins at Uxmal

Mayan ruins at Chichén Itzá

Mérida, the state capital

QUINTANA ROO

Tulum, the largest coastal city built by the Maya and the only Mayan city
    known to be inhabited when the Spaniards arrived

The Sian Ka'an Biosphere Reserve

Snorkeling and other water sports in beautiful Cozumel and Cancún

FURTHER READING

Chávez, Alicia Hernández. *Mexico: A Brief History*. Berkeley: University of California Press, 2006.

Franz, Carl, et al. *The People's Guide to Mexico*. Berkeley, Calif.: Avalon Travel Publishing, 2006.

Levy, Daniel C., and Kathleen Bruhn. *Mexico: The Struggle for Democratic Development*. Berkeley: University of California Press, 2006.

Meyer, Michael C., et al. *The Course of Mexican History*. New York: Oxford University Press, 2002.

Williams, Colleen Madonna Flood. *The Geography of Mexico*. Philadelphia: Mason Crest, 2009.

INTERNET RESOURCES

Mesoweb
http://www.mesoweb.com/welcome.html#externalresources

Mexico for Kids
http://www.elbalero.gob.mx/index_kids.html

Mexico Channel
http://www.mexicochannel.net

61

INDEX

63

PICTURE CREDITS

2:      ©OTTN Publishing

3:      Corbis Images

10:     Hulton/Archive

12:     Corbis Images

13:     Scala/Art Resource, NY

14:     Corbis Images

15:     Corbis Images

18:     Corbis Images

21:     Susan Kaye

23:     Corbis

27:     Susan Kaye

30:     Hulton/Archive

32:     Macduff Everton/Corbis

34:     Franz-Marc Frei/Corbis

35:     Corbis Images

37:     Corbis Images

38:     Jan Butchofsky-Houser/Houserstock

42:     Dave G. Houser/Houserstock

44:     Jan Butchofsky-Houser/Houserstock

45:     Jan Butchofsky-Houser/Houserstock

46:     Jan Butchofsky-Houser/Houserstock

47:     Hulton/Archive

48:     Macduff Everton/Corbis

51:     Dave G. Houser/Houserstock

52:     Susan Kaye

53:     Nik Wheeler/Corbis

54:     Corbis Images

Cover   (all, front and back) Used under license from Shutterstock, Inc.

CONTRIBUTORS

Roger E. Hernández is the most widely syndicated columnist writing on Hispanic issues in the United States. His weekly column, distributed by King Features, appears in some 40 newspapers across the country, including the *Washington Post*, *Los Angeles Daily News*, *Dallas Morning News*, *Arizona Republic*, *Rocky Mountain News* in Denver, *El Paso Times*, and *Hartford Courant*. He is also the author of *Cubans in America*, an illustrated history of the Cuban presence in what is now the United States, from the early colonists in 16th-century Florida to today's Castro-era exiles. The book was designed to accompany a PBS documentary of the same title.

Hernández's articles and essays have been published in the *New York Times*, *New Jersey Monthly*, *Reader's Digest*, and *Vista Magazine*; he is a frequent guest on television and radio political talk shows, and often travels the country to lecture on his topic of expertise. Currently, he is teaching journalism and English composition at the New Jersey Institute of Technology in Newark, where he holds the position of writer-in-residence. He is also a member of the adjunct faculty at Rutgers University.

Hernández left Cuba with his parents at the age of nine. After living in Spain for a year, the family settled in Union City, New Jersey, where Hernández grew up. He attended Rutgers University, where he earned a BA in Journalism in 1977; after graduation, he worked in television news before moving to print journalism in 1983. He lives with his wife and two children in Upper Montclair, New Jersey.

Randi Field is a freelance writer, editor, and lawyer in Silver Spring, Maryland. She has written numerous articles on law, science, and education for the American Bar Association's *Mental & Physical Disability* Law Reporter, the Smithsonian Institute's National Academy of Sciences, MedLearn, and WebMD. She practiced law for 11 years in Washington, D.C., in private practice and for the U.S. International Trade Commission and the Washington Legal Clinic for the Homeless. She has two children, Jared and Casey McGrath, both students at St. Bernadette School in Silver Spring.